THE ABC'S OF
GOLDFISH
KW-153

Contents

Photography: Dr. Herbert R. Axelrod, front and back endpapers, title page, 19, 53. Tom Caravaglia, 41. Michael Gilroy, 15, 39, 43 (top), 72, 81 (top), 89 (top). Andre Roth, 45, 63, 78, 83 (bottom), 85, 87. Edward C. Taylor, 11. R. Zukal, 51, 65. Photograph on page 73 courtesy of Kosmos Verlag. Photographs on pages 7, 9, 16, 17, 23, 25, 27, 29, 31, 33, 35, 57, 59, 61, 66, 67 (bottom), 71, 75, 77, 79, 81 (bottom), and 83 (top) courtesy of Midori Shobo, *Fish Magazine,* Japan. Photographs on pages 37 and 47 courtesy of Werther Paccagnella. Photograph on page 91 courtesy of Van Ness Water Gardens.

Drawings by John R. Quinn unless otherwise credited.

Distributed in the UNITED STATES by T.F.H. Publications, Inc., 211 West Sylvania Avenue, Neptune City, NJ 07753; in CANADA by H & L Pet Supplies Inc., 27 Kingston Crescent, Kitchener, Ontario N2B 2T6; Rolf C. Hagen Ltd., 3225 Sartelon Street, Montreal 382 Quebec; in ENGLAND by T.F.H. Publications Limited, 4 Kier Park, Ascot, Berkshire SL5 7DS; in AUSTRALIA AND THE SOUTH PACIFIC by T.F.H. (Australia) Pty. Ltd., Box 149, Brookvale 2100 N.S.W., Australia; in NEW ZEALAND by Ross Haines & Son, Ltd., 18 Monmouth Street, Grey Lynn, Auckland 2 New Zealand; in SINGAPORE AND MALAYSIA by MPH Distributors (S) Pte., Ltd., 601 Sims Drive, #03/07/21, Singapore 1438; in the PHILIPPINES by Bio-Research, 5 Lippay Street, San Lorenzo Village, Makati Rizal; in SOUTH AFRICA by Multipet Pty. Ltd., 30 Turners Avenue, Durban 4001. Published by T.F.H. Publications, Inc. Manufactured in the United States of America by T.F.H. Publications, Inc.

THE ABC'S OF
GOLDFISH
Neal Teitler

The Golden Fish

Goldfish vendor, from an ancient Oriental work of art.

Upon reviewing the history of the goldfish as it has been traced in the works of ancient and modern writers, the hobbyist is confronted with many obscure references. However, if these are considered carefully a fairly clear historical evolution of the goldfish can be revealed. With fact and fiction joining hands as the picture unfolds, we can trace their cultivation for close to a thousand years.

It was during the Tsin Dynasty (265-419 A.D.), some say, that a few red-scaled fish were first observed in China. But to say that these were our present golden-finned friends would be a misrepresentation. It is not until the Sung Dynasty (960-1279 A.D.) that we have any record of the goldfish's first domestication. By then the fish were being reared in ponds as household pets.

During the second Chin Dynasty (1115-1234 A.D.) the "Goldfish Pool" at **Peking was being used as a commercial breeding establishment. Indeed,** before 1276 A.D. varied colored goldfish were being bred and sold for pets in Hang-chow. So popular did they become that during the Ming Dynasty (1368-1643 A.D.) known for its pottery, goldfish were taken from their natural pools and cultivated in aquariums made of clay.

Apparently the Chinese maintained their monopoly on the chin-yii—their word for goldfish—for several hundred years. It is not until 1500 A.D. that we have any record of them in Japan. In 1704 we know that Sato Sanzaemon established a goldfish breeding business at Koriyama, which is still one of the great goldfish centers of the world.

Meanwhile, back in China, three new types of fancy chin-yii were being

6

The goldfish is an important element in many Oriental art motifs.

developed. Around 1590, double-tailed varieties (fantails) were first recorded. In 1621, transparent-scaled varieties were observed; one is depicted on a Chinese plate now in the possession of the British Museum. The publication of the Imperial encyclopedia, *T'u Shu*, in 1726, reveals the first picture of a goldfish lacking the dorsal fin.

Japan's preoccupation with the "golden fish" grew by leaps and bounds as newer varieties were produced and imported. In 1800, the ryukin was imported from the Ryukyu Islands, and at about this time the ranchu arrived from Korea. At a fish farm in Koriyama in 1840 a ryukin was bred with a ranchu, and this cross resulted in the oranda shishigashira.

Mr. K. Akiyama produced the shubunkin in 1900 by crossing two demekins; it was named by Mr. Matsubara. Mr. Akiyama also produced the calico ryukin; it was named by Mr. F. Packard in 1912. The demekin and demeranchu were introduced into Japan from China soon after the end of the Japanese-Chinese War in 1895.

On the other side of the world this natural oddity was also becoming popular. How did it get to Europe and then to America? Many tales were told about this Oriental wonder. In 1691 Petiver wrote the first valid account of this carp-like fish. By 1728 it was well-known in Europe. When Captain Philip Worth presented a large shipment of goldfish to Sir Mathew Decker in 1730, they were well on their way to popularity.

In 1750, the French East India Company brought them into France. The Netherlands in 1753 and Germany in 1780 were both introduced to this aquarist's delight. Edwards mentions

This closeup of a calico oranda shows the varying amounts of dark pigmentation in the skin and individual scales of the fish.

double-tailed goldfish in England in 1760. Veil-tails were first bred in France in 1873 and in Germany in 1883, but as early as 1772 Europe had become acquainted with the telescope (demekin) and the dorsal-less types. It was not until after the First World War that the shubunkin reached Europe.

While America probably saw its first goldfish in the early nineteenth century, Admiral Ammon's shipment of 1878 is recognized as the first major import. Before 1889 a goldfish farm was established near Frederick, Maryland; one still exists near there today. In 1899, Mr. Eugene Shireman founded a goldfish farm at Martinsville, Indiana.

The United States can lay claim to developing only one of the many varieties that exist today: the comet. It was apparently produced simultaneously by Hugo Mulertt and the U.S. Fisheries Department in 1881. Anyone who has watched the comet swim will agree that it was aptly named by Mr. Mulertt.

Other varieties are constantly being introduced. The celestial, bubble-eye, pearl-scale, pompon, and outfolded operculum are all twentieth century mutations. To say that this completes the goldfish's history is foolhardy because even today, with every spawning, some new variety may occur.

There are many different body shapes and color varieties among goldfish, but all goldfish belong to one species: *Carassius auratus*.

For generations, scientists have been studying evolution and, based on the work of Karl Linnaeus, the Swedish botanist, developing the science of taxonomy. This science has constructed a system of *taxa* (names) to explain the flow of evolution. The goldfish is listed accordingly:

KINGDOM: Animalia
PHYLUM: Chordata
SUBPHYLUM:
Vertebrata
CLASS: Osteichthyes
ORDER: Ostariophysi
FAMILY: Cyprinidae
GENUS: *Carassius*
SPECIES: *auratus*

Hence its name *Carassius auratus*.

Osteichthyes pertains to vertebrates (with a backbone) that have a swim bladder, paired pectoral and pelvic fins, an operculum, and possess an endo-skeleton (endo-internal) of bone and cartilage. The Ostariophysi are designated as those Osteichthyes having a series of small bones which connect the swim bladder to the ear. Cyprinidae have toothless jaws; this characterizes more than 2,000 species that belong to the family.

Carassius auratus, the goldfish, has one other member in its genus, the Crucian carp, *Carassius carassius.* The two are distinguished by basic differences in body shape and the convex dorsal fin margin of the Crucian carp versus the goldfish's straight or concave dorsal.

The wild form of the goldfish has between 28 and 31 scales along the lateral line and six scales between the dorsal spine and the lateral line. The goldfish has five sets of fins, and the variation in pairing characterizes different varieties. The swim bladder is an interesting adaptation to water; this is a paired organ in *Carassius auratus.* The swim bladder acts like a ballast tank, causing the fish to rise or sink in the water

The lionhead (bottom) lacks a dorsal fin, in contrast to the shubunkin (top).

as it wills.

This fish has five basic senses (sight, smell, taste, lateral line function, and memory) present in varying degrees. Sight is probably the weakest of the goldfish's senses, but coupled with the smell and lateral line adaptations, swift, sharp motions can be made to react to food or other stimuli. The lateral line is a series of pits along the fish's side and is basically an element of touch. When vibrations of the water occur, no matter how slight, a pressure is exerted on this line. Since thermo-sensory nerve endings occur along its length, it is assumed that hot and cold can also be detected by this organ.

To understand the scale groups and coloration of the goldfish, an examination is necessary to explain the reason for their occurrence. Fish have a set of pigment cells called chromatophores which react to temperature, composition of the water,

and other environmental factors. Two types which are found in the goldfish are melanophores and xanthophores. In the wild fish an even distribution of both is noted. The yellow and orange types lack the melanophores (black bodies), while in the blue type the xanthophores are absent. Guanine deposited in the cells causes the reflective tissue to be bluish gray in color. A fish's scale group is determined by how much guanine is present at what depth in the skin and scales.

The nomenclature of scale groups developed by the Goldfish Society of Great Britain is the best available:

METALLIC: One that has a lot of guanine and is, therefore, as highly reflective as polished metal.

MATT: The term used to describe fish having a translucent or flat coloration. No matter how closely you examine them, no reflective tissue can be found, not even in the eye

orbit, which is an intense black.

NACREOUS: A hybrid of the first two, showing signs of both. Some scales, organs, or other areas might show a concentration of guanine-laden reflective tissue.

CALICO: Originally referred to nacreous fish but is now used to describe a fish of any group which has three or more colors scattered over the body haphazardly, usually including blue. The better calico has regions of intense blue scales.

Scaled and scaleless are useless terms because they are not exact enough, do not explain the hybrid type, and are improper since all goldfish have scales.

The magnificent calico oranda shishigashira.

— *Varieties* —

There are many varieties of goldfish. Considering the number of variations in fins, color, body shape, etc., that are possible, the number would appear astronomical. Fortunately, however, the combinations accepted as valid varieties are small when compared to this theoretical number. All goldfish varieties existing today stem from the original stocks developed by Chinese, Korean, and Japanese breeders.

Names are a hard thing to pin down. Each culture, and sometimes regions in that culture, calls the same fish by different names. Oriental breeders look for different features than do those in the western world. It is because of this that some of their names have no English translation. The Chinese use the name dragon to refer to types for which we find no basis. In contrast, the American and British cannot even agree on common English names.

Taking into account contemporary nomenclature, anatomy, and genetics, as well as general descriptiveness, I have set down names which I feel fit the recognized types. Before describing them I will try to explain the recognized variations which when combined form the established breeds.

Color

As previously noted, the depth and intensity of the guanine layer will determine the scale group in which the fish is placed. The chromatophores which are distributed above the guanine, over the skin, determine the coloration. Often these cells expand or contract under visual or nervous stimuli, allowing intensity and sometimes color to change. Darkness tends to cause the chromatophores to expand, thereby amplifying the fish's color. Besides the melanophores (black) and

The telescope goldfish, with its protruding eyes, is a mutation of the fantail.

the xanthophores (yellow-orange), deep orange and violet coloring cells have been found. Currently blue is being examined closely to discover if it could be another type.

Fish coloring varies according to the number and size of the chromatophores present. Black, brown, and the wild green are caused by different combinations of the black and yellow pigment cells. Blue goldfish occur in two ways. The blue can be caused by a large amount of guanine and the absence of orange, with some black, or by the black pigmentation lying further down in the skin, with little or no guanine present.

Red or orange specimens occur when few or no black chromatophores are present. Silver or white specimens occur when no pigmentation appears in the skin and only guanine is present. An albino lacks pigment everywhere, including the eyes, which are pink. It

should be noted that an albino goldfish is not white but pale orange in color. The late Professor Shishan C. Chen noted that no albino goldfish had appeared up to the time of his famous paper in 1925. Today, albino types of most varieties are being raised everywhere.

Almost all, if not all, types of pigment cells and kinds of reflecting tissues present in domesticated goldfish occur in wild specimens. In the latter, however, the cells are distributed more evenly and rarely in so great a concentration as to produce red, orange, blue, or other colored spots. The color cells and reflecting layers in the wild form are so distributed that the fish is gray, dull olive, silvery white, or shades of these in various parts of its body. So, in a sense, the domesticated goldfish has nothing new in terms of color that the parent wild form did not have. However, through

Peacocktail (*top*); ranchu (*bottom*), also known as a lionhead.

change of the genetic material that governs the distribution and concentration of pigment cells, nature has altered the goldfish to produce our brightly colored domesticated varieties.

Finnage

This is an over-all term used to describe the five sets of fins which appear on the fish. Variation in finnage occurs basically in three ways: by doubling or pairing of caudal and anal fins, by their absence (mainly with reference to the dorsal fins), and by an increase in length (all fins, especially caudals).

CAUDAL OR TAIL FIN: The caudal fin varies greatly among the many varieties. This structure consists of a flat membrane supported by fin rays. It develops from a single tail (two-lobed) to the doubled or bilaterally-paired fins (four-lobed). In prize fish the double caudals should be separated all the way to the base or root of the tail, of equal size (especially the lobes), and without permanent folds.

ANAL FIN: As in the caudal, the anal can develop into long or short, single or double types. Double-tail (fan-tail) varieties must have double anals, and they should be of equal size.

DORSAL FIN: When considering the dorsal one rule holds true: it should be all there or there should be no trace at all. The breeds lacking the dorsal should have a smooth back covered evenly with scales, with no vestigial stump showing. A variety with a dorsal should keep it erect, having no folds or breaks evident. In the highly prized veil-tail a sure sign of a good fish is its extremely high dorsal standing like a sail against the wind.

PELVIC AND PECTORAL FINS: These fins also vary in size and shape according to the breed. All of these should be

— *Varieties* —

paired and straight, having a symmetrical appearance.

Body Shape

Observation of the many pictures in this book indicates the drastic variations in body shape. It is startling to realize that the very short-bodied veil-tail is an indirect mutation from the long-bodied common goldfish. One "must" for any good specimen is that it must be symmetrical and not distorted.

Head

The hooded goldfish varieties are becoming more popular than ever; they can, therefore, be found in most large pet shops. A good growth does not usually appear until at least the third year. Head shape also varies from pointed to blunt (or square). Oriental breeders have in the past placed more emphasis on this than have those in the West. Head shape is important and it should be

taken into account according to the variety.

Other Mutations

Globe or telescope eyes occur and form distinctive types. Nasal growths have been propagated to form another breed. In some fish the bony operculum is affected so another type has come into being.

Varieties

A general rule applied to describe the origin of the many breeds is as follows: Chinese breeders select for grotesque shapes and appearance; the Japanese select for that which is graceful, flowing, and esthetically pleasing. The names I have chosen from the past writings are those which best describe their types.

Tail Types

This variety is called either "edojikin" or "kujaku," which means peacock.

SINGLE-TAIL

This is the least modified of ornamental goldfish, having a body shape and fin structure similar to that of the wild type. These were the first cultivated goldfish bred by the Chinese. They are the easiest variety to breed and the hardiest. Outdoors in a pool they grow to 12 inches in two years. After a number of years, lake-grown "commons" can grow close to two feet. A calico, matt, or nacreous common is usually called a shubunkin.

Comet (tetsugyo)

The comet is a long-finned common goldfish said to have originated about 1880 in United States Government ponds on the Mall in Washington, D.C. Hugo Mulertt, a pioneer American breeder, may have also originated this fish at about the same time; at any rate, he gave it its name.

The body of a fine comet is more elongated than that of the common goldfish and the single tail-fin as long as, or preferably longer than, the body. All other fins are at least twice the length of those of the common goldfish and often, and preferably, much longer.

Like the common goldfish it is a hardy fish well able to stand cold winters outdoors, and it is a prolific and efficient breeder. It is a graceful, active fish and its fins do not seem as delicate and subject to disease as do other long-finned varieties. It can reach a length of 20 inches but ordinarily reaches 14 inches in outdoor pools. It makes an excellent ornamental pond fish as it is better able to escape small boys, cats, and other predators than can the double-tailed, short-bodied varieties.

London and Bristol shubunkins

These fish are recognized solely as shubunkins or calicoes of other types. The

The ryukin goldfish, also known as the fantail. This fish is about five years old.

London shubunkin resembles the common fish in body and finnage. As mentioned previously, it is basically a calico type of the matt or nacreous fish. The Bristol shubunkin resembles the comet in body shape and long square finnage. In most respects it is like the Goldfish Society's single-tail variety except that its tail is square at the ends instead of rounded.

DOUBLE-TAIL
Ribbon-tail (fan-tail, ryukin)

A short body and fairly long finnage typify this group. Smaller finnage as found in the commercial fan-tail is really an inferior form of ryukin. Poor culling results in fish with longer bodies and short fins as found in the wakin. The longer the body of a fish, the more chance you have of obtaining a single-tail in your future spawns. Most often the good specimens will grow to about ten inches in three years.

According to its recorded history, the ryukin originally came from the Ryukyu Islands. The best ribbon-tails have deeply divided tails (four lobes), two anals, and a complete division of the two caudals down to the base.

Veil-tail (twin-tail)

High dorsals, long finnage, and "square cut" caudals make this fish the aristocrat of the goldfish family. Good specimens are hard to come by and command high prices. In all cases the caudal and anals are doubled and must be divided down to the base; they must be symmetrical. This is one of the least hardy of the varieties, so care must be taken when handling them. Their short body and long finnage slow them down, making them easy prey for outdoor predators. Many times their tail grows too long and must

be trimmed (tail-docking) a procedure recommended by the noted goldfish expert Mr. J. W. Anderson.

An excellent specimen may breed only one or two squared tails, so care must be taken in order to raise them. A good sign of a good fish is one that has a very high dorsal with extremely long finnage. The square tail comes later or can be bred out in later generations.

Globe-eye (telescope, demekin, chair-lay)

For years these fish have been called "telescope," a name which is very inappropriate. The protruding eyes which characterize this group are anything but telescopic. Body shape should be short and the fins symmetrically paired. Eye shape varies in four ways. A good specimen has long fins and a well-divided ribbon-tail. Coloration varies immensely, creating the varying types of demekins which the Japanese have named.

Black Moor (kuro demekin)

A type of globe-eye, this fish is solid black in color, preferably with a matt covering. Many Moors turn color later in age, since black is the least stable of goldfish colors. Mr. Anderson states that a Moor with a white or silvery belly will remain black, while one with a brassy or golden belly will turn orange later in its life.

Pearl-scale (chee-lun)

Of all the modern varieties (those produced after 1900) this has proved extremely popular. Its body is extremely short and round, approaching a softball in size and shape. The scales seem like hemispheres or half pearls which have been pasted onto the fish's body. Good specimens have large scales and short square finnage. Young fry with

Tail Types

A velvetyball with narial
bouquets.

ribbon-tail caudals can later
develop into fish with
square veil-tails.

It is interesting to note
that when a scale is injured
and falls off the new scale is
of the normal flat type, but
this does not affect the fish's
breeding ability to transfer
genes for good pearl-scaled
development to its progeny.

Oranda

Goldfish hobbyists and
breeders are all agreed that
the oranda is a fish universal
in appeal. A good specimen
has a well-developed hood (a
puffy growth of the skin in
the head region), long paired
finnage, a high dorsal, and a
well-developed short body.
Oranda shishigashira is used
mainly to refer to the type
of oranda which has only a
well-developed cap. The
azumanishiki is the Japanese
name for a calico oranda, a
name widely used all over
the world. Some orandas
grow to 12 inches and
appear to do well when
wintered outdoors. Top

specimens, however, if more
than five years old, should
be taken indoors during the
winter period.

Bramblehead (lionhead, ranchu, shetau)

The Bramblehead has a
short round body, short
finnage, no dorsal, a double
anal fin, and a warty growth
on the head. Specimens
should have no dorsal
vestiges, and the back can
either be slightly rounded
with caudal straight out or
fairly flat with the caudal
peduncle and caudals at a
45° inclination downward.
Three hood types are
recognized by the Japanese:
tokin—growth only on cap;
okame—swollen-cheeked;
shishigashira—full hood on
cap, cheeks, and opercular
region.

Pompon (yeung-kau)

The variety recognized
today lacks the dorsal. (The
Japanese type, hanafusa, has
it, and many people have
incorrectly called it

Since 1952, *Tropical Fish Hobbyist* has been the source of accurate, up-to-the-minute, and fascinating information on every facet of the aquarium hobby. Join the more than 50,000 devoted readers world-wide who wouldn't miss a single issue.

...From T.F.H., the world's largest publisher of bird books, a new bird magazine for birdkeepers all over the world...

CAGED BIRD HOBBYIST
IS FOR EVERYONE
WHO LOVES BIRDS.

CAGED BIRD HOBBYIST
IS PACKED WITH VALUABLE
INFORMATION SHOWING HOW
TO FEED, HOUSE, TRAIN AND CARE
FOR ALL TYPES OF BIRDS.

Subscribe right now so you don't miss a single copy!   SM-316

Tail Types

Water bubble-eyes, or frogheads
as they are called in Japanese,
have been developed in recent
years.

Pompon, but a more apt
name advocated by Professor
Chen is narial bouquet.) All
finnage is paired, the body
is short, and the nasal
appendages are folded many
times to form tufts. As with
all goldfish lacking a dorsal,
short finnage is preferred so
that the fish are able to
move and balance with some
ease.

Celestial (deme ranchu, chiu-tien ngarn, chotengan)

This grotesque variation
of the globe-eye was
probably produced in Korea
sometime after 1780,
winding up in Japan about
1901. Characteristic of this
breed are the upturned eyes
encased in a hard bulbous
orbit. These fish, which lack
a dorsal fin, are extremely
delicate and can be easily
injured. All sharp objects
should be removed from the
tank because they are able to
see only upward. Feeding
with prepared fish foods
which will not cloud the
water or decay rapidly is
especially necessary for this
variety.

Bubble-eye

Another grotesque
Chinese production, the
bubble-eye is extremely
delicate. The eyeball is quite
normal, but large fluid-filled
sacs protrude from the eye
socket, causing the eyeball
to turn up almost as much
as does the celestial's. Good
specimens have a short
body, paired finnage (short),
no dorsal, and extremely
large fluid sacs equal to each
other in size. This variety
was first described by
Professor Chen and is
believed to be a twentieth
century mutation.

Other types

The outfolded operculum
(faan si) is a popular
Chinese fish which is
seldom seen outside of
China. Good specimens
have a high dorsal, good
ribbontail, long paired
finnage, and operculum

Setting Up

folded back on both sides, exposing the gills.

Albinos are now being bred in most varieties. According to Chen no one had seen an albino prior to 1925. The American breeders have developed strains that are available in limited quantities.

Other varieties not yet mentioned include: the nymph, a single-tailed ryukin; the blue Moor; the brown or chocolate variety; and the red cap oranda which is all white with red only on the shishigashira cap. The egg-fish is a type which was popular in the United States for a while but is now bred only in limited numbers in China.

Selecting the tank

When starting out to buy the aquarium, keep in mind that it is to serve as a *home* for your goldfish and do not consider it as just a fancy decoration. Goldfish require more space than most varieties of pet fish. To begin with, a safe rule to follow is to allow one inch of fish (not including the tail) per gallon of water. Since the goldfish needs a good supply of oxygen, no less than 30 square inches of surface area is required for each inch of fish. Surface area can be determined by multiplying the length of the tank by its width. Gallon capacity can be found by using the formula:

$$\frac{\text{Length x Width x Height}}{231}$$

All measurements are in inches.

Now that we have determined the size, let's consider the shape of the tank. The aquarium best suited to goldfish is one which is rectangular. Squat

All goldfish—but especially young fish such as those in the lower photo—require clean, well oxygenated water.

bowls or turtle bowls, while not bad in a pinch, should be avoided. Glass bowls shaped like globes or like a layer-cake on its side are not too good either, but if you are determined to have one remember this: under no circumstances fill the bowl *above* the widest portion, usually its half-way point. While most of these glass bowls are inexpensive, in the long run they cause more trouble than the saving is worth.

Many beginners decide to start small and then get larger tanks. If you can afford only a small tank, try to spend a little more and buy at least a ten-gallon aquarium. I have observed novices who count fish size and then buy a five-gallon tank. Before long they see some other fish that they would like to have but make the sad discovery that their tank will not hold them. If in doubt, always buy the larger tank. If you have a choice between two

tanks with the same capacity, differing only in length and width, choose the one with the larger surface area.

Choose an aquarium made by a well-known firm. You will then have a tank that will stand up under use. Above all, remember that a reputable dealer who sells well-known brands is a dealer you can rely on.

When you have gotten your tank home and set in place, your job has just begun. Fill the tank with about two inches of water and wait for half an hour. Examine the tank, checking for any small leaks. Small drips are usually sealed by water pressure at that point inside the aquarium. Larger leaks must be cared for *immediately*. Empty the tank, let it dry, and then get to work with a good silicone cement. The key to solving most tank problems is experimentation: try some established method and then judge for yourself.

The TropiQuarium unit from Rolf C. Hagen Corp. combines heating, filtration and lighting equipment all within one compact aquarium-and-full-hood unit that operates from the unit's single electrical plug.

Setting Up

Goldfish really deserve better treatment than to be restricted to small bowls; they'll eventually suffer in such cramped quarters.

Location

The placement of your tank should be carefully considered. No direct sunlight must hit it. A tank staying too long in the sun turns green with algae quickly and presents a problem. Indirect sunlight or artificial lighting for about six hours a day is enough. If there are plants in the tank, then the lighting should be for at least ten hours. With plants you can gauge the amount of light needed because if they do not get enough they will begin to turn brown.

Gravel—yes or no?

Gravel is a big "if" in keeping goldfish. If you decide to use gravel, its size is extremely important. Bits that are too large cause accumulation of dirt and wastes which can result in disease. Bits that are too small cause bacteria to form, blackening the packed bottom layer. What is the right size? From past experience I would say those bits of gravel about three-eighths to one-fourth inch in size are about best. One and a half pounds of this size gravel for each gallon of tank capacity are more than ample.

I must warn any novice that goldfish do not keep the best of company with plants and gravel. This fish is a scavenger and will rearrange the bottom of the tank at will. One time I discovered 20 pounds of gravel moved to one corner of the tank in less than two days. You can become quite disturbed if after carefully planting and aquascaping a new tank you see all your effort gone to waste.

Water

Most water is chlorinated and/or fluoridated and therefore must be conditioned. There are chemicals on the market for this purpose, but letting the water stand for 24 hours is a satisfactory method. pH or

alkalinity-acidity of the water is not an important factor with goldfish. After the fish have lived for a while in the water, it usually becomes slightly acid.

Water hardness, while important for tropical fishes, can vary with goldfish. It should be noted, however, that in commercial fisheries before the fish are shipped they are conditioned by being placed in a pond filled with spring water which is hard and slightly alkaline.

Once your tank is filled, don't under any circumstances move it.

Pumps

The pump is one item which will be determined by your individual set-up. Here you have a wide choice in styles, types, and capacity. Two basic types are available: the vibrator or diaphragm pump and the piston pump.

Vibrator pumps are less expensive and have mechanical failures less often than do the piston pumps. This pump works by way of a rubber diaphragm which is actuated by a mechanism similar to that operating an electric bell or buzzer. For a beginner, this is probably the best. Later on, however, you may want to set up a series of five or more tanks. With a system this large, the vibrator pump is inadequate and a piston pump will be needed.

The piston pump operates through a motor system. A magnet inside changes with the AC current, causing a small rod to rotate. This rod is connected to a wheel by way of a belt, and the wheel is connected to a plunger. The plunger, which is inside a cylindrical case, moves up and down, forcing air down into the cylinder and out through a connection to the air line. Most piston pumps must be cleaned and oiled regularly according to the maker's directions.

Here, as always, if the

Vibrator air pumps vary in size and power; the Rolf C. Hagen Corp. vibrators shown here are designed to handle the smallest aquariums right up to some of the largest standard sizes.

This bright-colored young oranda shows fine form in its variegated tail.

pump is purchased from a reputable dealer and is one made by a well-known company, you stand a good chance that your pump will cause few or no problems. Most economy pumps create nothing more than breakdowns. While a pump with a guarantee may cost more, the cost is low when you consider how long it will be in use.

Filters

Several types can be recommended for the goldfish tank. The outside power filter is perhaps the best as it is the easiest to clean and takes up no room in the aquarium, which is important in tanks of less than 15-gallon capacity. When the floss which acts as a filter becomes dirty, the air line is stopped and the floss is replaced. Thus, after only a few minutes of interrupted service, the filter is back at work. The outside filter does have one disadvantage, however. If

the water level drops too low, it ceases operation.

In many tanks a corner filter is used in conjunction with an outside filter. While the outside filter cleans up most wastes along the bottom of the aquarium, the bottom filter will remove most floating wastes. It is easy to clean but it must be removed from the tank to do so. When you replace the floss be extremely careful that no fibers remain outside the cover. I have seen this carelessness cause the death of many a goldfish: when the fish sees the glistening floss it tugs at it and either chokes on it or swallows it. The chief fault of the corner filter is that it takes up space in the tank.

With any of these filters, set up and cleaning is an easy task. The charcoal that is purchased from pet shops is often dusty and should be rinsed. Place the charcoal in a pail under a faucet. Run the water until the overflow is crystal clear, making sure

Glass bowls like this one do
more harm than good; aquariums
are recommended.

that you agitate the charcoal
four or five times. A more
efficient method is to use a
sixteenth-inch mesh net. Fill
the net three-quarters full of
charcoal and agitate it under
running water by pressing
up the bottom several times.
When you see that a clear
flow of water is running
through, you will know that
the charcoal is clean. Wash
the filter and place this
clean charcoal in it, filling it
a third of the way. Add floss
to the two-thirds mark, and
your filter is ready to
operate.

Undergravel filters are
often used in conjunction
with power filters, especially
in larger aquaria. They are
slotted plastic plates that go
under the gravel layer. Your
dealer will gladly show you
the best type of filter for
your aquarium set-up.

Air stone

An air stone is another
useful item because it allows
more water to be exposed to
the air. Air stone bubbles do

not add oxygen to the water
directly; they stir up the
water, causing a faster
exchange of oxygen at the
surface with the carbon
dioxide in the water.

Valves

When you set up an air
system of more than one
filter or aerator, you will
have to consider the valve
system. The two types
available include one which
is a series of valves with one
inflow and many outflows
and one composed of a
series of three-way valves. I
have tested both and prefer
the former. All the valve
controls are on one gang
valve, making it easy to
control and adjust each unit
to the desired air outflow.

Other accessories

The goldfish hobbyist will
also find these things useful:
a dip tube or siphon tube, a
feeding ring, a net, and a
thermometer.

As for the siphon tube, I
have found the best way to

Goldfish will accept food at all
levels in the tank, although they
scour the bottom more avidly.

clean dirt from the tank is
with a length of ordinary
tubing. Cut a piece of air
hose about four feet long.
Attach it to a wooden dowel,
which should be about six
inches longer than the depth
of your tank, so that one
end of the tubing sticks out
about half an inch beyond
the end. Place this end in
the water and either suck up
water or lay the entire piece
of tubing under the water
until all the air escapes and
it is filled. Put your finger
on the loose end and set it
in a bucket *lower* than the
bottom of the tank. Now
move the other end along
the bottom of your tank at
about a 60° angle until all
waste products are sucked
up. Anything too large to
pass through the tube
should be avoided and
picked up later with a net.
The siphon flow is stopped
simply by lifting the tip of
the hose out of the tank.
Aged water is then added to
the tank, replacing the
quantity siphoned out.

A feeding ring set in one
place keeps the food in the
same spot, training the fish
to know where it will be
found. The net, of course, is
used to handle the fish,
moving them from one tank
to another or into medicated
water for treatment. An
inexpensive thermometer is
needed as a guide to
checking aged water that is
being added to the tank or
the water in a tank to which
the fish are being moved. A
heater is not necessary
unless you intend to raise
fry.

Introducing the fish

Once your tank has been
washed and rinsed with salt
and all the necessary things
have been added to it
(including plants if you so
desire), check the
temperature, comparing it
with the water the fish are
now in. If your water has
been properly aged (or
chemically treated) and the
temperature variation of the
water is 5°F or less, you

This rooted plant, *Sagittaria*, multiplies rapidly, usually by means of runners.

may add your goldfish and sit back and admire your creation.

PLANTS, GRAVEL

Except for show purposes, most goldfish aquarists discourage the use of gravel and plants. But for those who can't be discouraged, I mention here those plants best able to stand abuse. These varieties are all good oxygenators and are to be found in most pet shops. When buying plants, look for those which are a vivid green, upright, not wilted, and, last but not least, with few or no brown-tipped leaves. As a guide, the various plants have been divided into three general groups: rooted, bunched, and floaters.

Rooted

These do best when planted and the roots are allowed to sprout and settle. *Vallisneria, Sagittaria,* and Amazon swords are the three best for the goldfish aquarium. All of these send out new plants by means of runners. Under good growing conditions (usually not with goldfish) they will multiply rapidly, producing dense jungles of underwater growth. *Vallisneria* comes in many forms and shapes. It is thin and tall, sometimes twining like a corkscrew. It is an excellent oxygenator. It varies in height from six inches to several feet and in width is about one-quarter of an inch. This plant is unusually hardy and thrives under even extreme conditions.

Sagittaria resembles *Vallisneria* in size and shape. Its leaves are slightly broader and, while tougher, are more brittle. Usually it multiplies rapidly and supplies a good deal of oxygen. Once *Sagittaria* begins to brown, cut off the tips or, if necessary, the whole leaf. In most aquaria *Sagittaria* roots easily, spreading out to obtain a firm foothold.

Lagarosiphon major with good lighting can turn a luxuriant green and makes an attractive addition to the tank.

Sword plants, especially the Amazon variety, are as close to ideal goldfish aquarium plants as one can hope to get. They establish themselves easily and, once set, multiply at a slow but steady pace. With good lighting they turn a luxuriant green and make an attractive addition to the tank. No matter how much the goldfish work on them, sword plants seem to be able to withstand their abuse.

Bunched

This group is always to be found where goldfish are bred and raised. Outdoors nothing can compare with them. In a tank they can prove useful, but they are also a hazard. The bunch plants usually do not have true roots and reproduce by means of branches forming off the main stem. They are quite brittle, and with active fish they may end up as a pile of rotting plant fragments.

Elodea has a main stem which grows to anywhere from four inches to four feet. The leaves form whorls, a circle around the stem, and are thin, flat, and pointed at the tip. Goldfish eat the leaves readily and can strip the stem in a matter of minutes. Scientific studies on plant respiration have shown *Elodea* to be one of the best oxygenators. Old growth tends to be brown and should be cut off. Cuttings of the stems will form new plants.

Cabomba, popular outdoors, has only mild success inside. It is composed of very fine fan-like leaves usually paired around the stem. It is quite brittle, and goldfish have a tendency to thrash it to bits. In spite of these problems, *Cabomba* is internationally famous as an ideal breeding plant. For an unusual effect, try the red variety.

Ambulia is a fairly recent introduction. Its color varies between green and red; it is sometimes mistaken for

Aquarium stores have some very
beautiful aquarium set-ups for
your home or office.

Cabomba. More careful
examination will show it to
be more dense and rubbery
in texture. Under the right
growing conditions it fares
better than *Cabomba,* even
in tanks.

Floaters

Of the many types of
floating plants only four will
be mentioned here. *Azolla,
Salvinia, Riccia,* and
duckweed are the most
popular and easy to acquire.
In general, the floating
plants have roots, are flat,
and multiply quickly. They
require plenty of light and
more than ample growing
area. If they run out of
spreading room they tend to
double up and rise out of
the water.

Azolla is native to the
southern states of the U.S.
and is found mainly in bog-
like areas. Its colors range
anywhere from bright green
to deep crimson. In
appearance it resembles
miniature spinach or
evergreen leaves

approximately half an inch
in length. As with most
floaters, *Azolla* requires a lot
of sun.

Salvinia is considered by
many to be the star of
floating plants. Besides
giving shade in ponds, it
provides a vegetable food
source for goldfish. *Salvinia*
is oval in shape with fine
hairs extending up from its
leaves to form a moss-like
texture.

Riccia is another plant
which requires intense
sunlight. It is a vivid green
sponge-like mass which
intertwines while floating
just beneath the surface. In
some cases, aquarists have
rid ponds of *Riccia* because
it looks something like a
stringy variety of algae.

Duckweed or *Lemna*
appears in dense numbers
on ponds. In general, it
looks like a miniature
version of the oval-shaped
Salvinia. However, it lacks
Salvinia's fine hairs and
grows in separate leaves or
groups of three and four,

Champion ranchu lionhead goldfish from Japan. The larger the head growth, the older the fish.

while *Salvinia* leaves lie on the same stem in groups of seven and up. Duckweed is known all over the world because it establishes itself easily in streams and ponds. Some hobbyists have noticed that the leaves when eaten by goldfish tend to have a slight laxative effect.

Gravel

Gravel when purchased is usually not clean. To clean it, use the cleaning method for charcoal discussed in the section on filters. Make sure that any gravel is washed thoroughly before it is put into the aquarium because the scum its dust will form on the surface is unsightly and hard to remove. The gravel should be placed in cleaned flower pots or behind a barrier. A strong salt solution can be used to clean the pots and other equipment—be sure to carefully rinse it off, of course.

The flower pot method is an efficient way of setting up your tank. Plants which need treatment can then be removed easily, while re-planting will not disturb the water. My experience is that goldfish will not bother potted plants as readily as they do those planted directly in gravel.

The barrier method is perhaps the best, and it works two ways: it keeps the plants and gravel safe, and it makes clean-up easier. Use a sheet of glass or Plexiglas cut to fit the inside length of the aquarium and with holes perforating the outside edges. Place this vertically about four inches from the rear of the tank to serve as a partition. Behind it place the gravel and arrange the plants. The holes will allow an exchange of gases between the two areas, but they should be too small to give the goldfish access to the plants. When the plants are well-rooted, flourishing, and better able to withstand the fish's abuse, this barrier can, if desired, be removed.

A champion-quality stock of Nagoya goldfish called "jikin," or peacocktail goldfish.

If the usual method of laying gravel is used, slope it down toward the front. With the barrier method or with the plants in pots, water can be poured directly into the area where there is no planting. If not, newspaper should be laid over the gravel, a saucer placed on top of it, and the water poured slowly onto the saucer until the tank is filled. If this method is used, the plants, of course, will not be added until all the water is in and the newspaper carefully removed.

There are many different foods available for goldfish; most are inexpensive and easy to obtain. The greater the variety, the more active and colorful your fish will become. Dried and/or pelleted foods, frozen foods, mixed pastes, and live foods are all available. Nothing, in my opinion, beats the last.

Dried foods that are high in starch content tend to cloud the water. New flake foods have been developed which do not foul the tank as readily, and the fish seem to find them appetizing. Shrimp pellets are high in animal matter and have a sharp smell easily detected by the fish. While dried foods have their use, they should not be fed to the exclusion of frozen or live foods. Paste mixtures are made up with different foods like liver, spinach, and egg. Freeze-dried and deep-frozen foods are also available in a wide variety of types at your pet dealer.

Live foods should form

the foundation of your feeding schedule. They provide goldfish with foods similar to those they eat in their natural surroundings. Again the choice is great, giving you complete freedom to choose the one best suited to your requirements.

Daphnia

These small crustaceans are also known as water fleas. If you are adventurous, you can search for them in nearby lakes and ponds. It is a food, however, that should be fed in moderation because its chitinous shell acts as a laxative.

If a successful culture can be established, you have a ready supply of live food. Start the culture by placing about an inch of rich organic soil into a jar of stagnant water and letting it stand in the sun for several days. A good algal growth is necessary; it can be stimulated by the addition of

some nitrate and phosphate. When the water is ready, add some daphnia. Give them at least a week to establish themselves. It is best to raise several cultures simultaneously because fluctuations and constant use will deplete the original culture.

Brine shrimp

Whole books have been written on this tiny crustacean. They inhabit the Great Salt Lake as well as other areas of high salt concentration and have brought into being a thriving industry. They can be purchased live from most pet shops or can be grown from eggs at home.

Establish a culture by taking a bottle like a cider or wine jug and cutting off the bottom. The tightly corked bottle is then turned upside down and an aerator stone placed in the neck. Salt water in a concentration of about 12 ounces of salt per gallon of water is added.

Many aquarists add two ounces of Epsom salts and one ounce of sodium bicarbonate as well. A temperature of 75°F. is best. The eggs hatch in one or two days. The shrimp can be fed on brewer's yeast.

I find brine shrimp to be one of the best foods, carrying no diseases and stimulating the activity of the fish.

Tubifex

This thin long red worm is found in swamp-like areas. As a food for growing fry, nothing can compare with it. The major objection is that they are sometimes said to carry disease. They can be purchased in aquarium shops and should be kept in shallow water under a dripping faucet for at least 12 hours before feeding. Since their culture at home is difficult I do not recommend it.

Microworms

These tiny worms, white to beige in color, can also be purchased at your pet shop with instructions on how to culture them with oatmeal and a few other ingredients. When fry have reached the two-week stage this serves as an excellent food. A word of caution: if the culture turns sour, throw it out: don't re-use the worms.

Drosophila

The fruitfly is now taking its place among the popular goldfish foods. It is small (about one-fourth inch) and easy to cultivate. Of the many varieties only the wingless (vestigial) is of practical use. Your culture must be kept closed to prevent any wild flies from entering.

A simple culture can be made by boiling water, adding it to agar agar, and then adding some mashed banana. It is put in a jar and allowed to jell. Then a few fruitflies are added. Within two weeks you will have fruitflies to feed to your

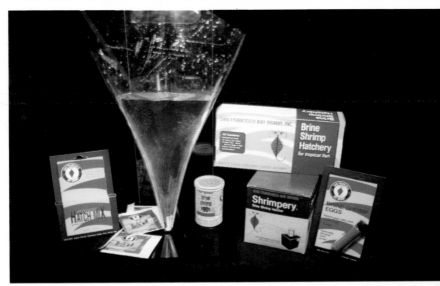

The equipment and supplies necessary to hatch brine shrimp for feeding to baby fish are available at well stocked pet shops and tropical fish specialty stores. The eggs, hatching mix and hatching equipment shown here are from San Francisco Bay Brand.

Recently a white cap Oranda has been developed.

Inspect all live plants before introducing them into your tank because they could be a potential source of pests.

fish. Several jars should be started so that a new supply is constantly available.

The two Rolf C. Hagen Corp. products shown here represent two different types of prepared foods: one (above) that is formulated specifically for use with goldfish and one formulated for all aquarium fish but eagerly accepted by goldfish.

Many health problems derive from crowding, overfeeding, and fouling by waste materials. When any disease is identified it is as important to get rid of the source as it is to treat the fish. Disinfect the tank if more than one fish develops trouble.

On the following pages, I have charted common ailments and some ways to treat them. There are other methods but those given are the ones that I know work. Potassium permanganate and metallic copper are effective medications but they must be used with extreme caution. They can kill the fish they are supposed to cure. In most cases I do not recommend them to the novice. He is better off if he uses the reliable remedies purchasable at aquarium supply stores.

It is usually safe to assume that a diseased fish was weak before it was attacked. Most foes are airborne and

will not attack a fish until its resistance is down. If you keep your tank clean, your fish healthy, and you isolate newcomers and perform periodic checks, you will rarely meet any of these problems. An ounce of prevention is always worth a pound of cure.

Wounds should be swabbed with 5% methylene blue every 12 hours for two days; this will keep fungus from taking hold.

Beyond all else in keeping goldfish healthy, the aquarium should have daily cleaning if possible; if not, at least every other day. Decaying matter, an overabundance of algae, or just poor maintenance can lower the resistance of your fish until they are easy victims for their foes. A well-rounded diet of live food, frozen food, pastes, and dried preparations will do much to produce fine healthy fish, brighten their colors, and enhance their beauty. Every other month

one tablespoon of aquarium salt for each ten gallons of water should be added to the tank to stimulate the fish and lessen the chances of infection. Extensive water changes and constant dipping of the hands into the tank should both be avoided.

This black froghead is so topheavy that it must rest in this position with its head on the gravel.

Diseases

The shape of some goldfish varieties makes the fish look permanently swollen with eggs.

FISH FOES

Name	Symptoms	Treatment
Gill Fluke *(Dactylogyrus)*	Gills swell up, with a pus-like substance exuded around the area. (Prevalent among fry.) Fish gasp for air.	Fish are placed in a 2-quart-container; 10 drops of formaldehyde are added to the water; then 10 more drops are added every minute for the next 10 minutes. If fish shows any discomfort remove it. Repeat daily for the next 3 days. For fry, add 6 tblsp. of rock salt per quart of water. Dip fry in this for 30 seconds; then place them in a disinfected tank. Repeat in one hour for a final treatment.
Skin Fluke *(Gyrodactylus)*	Fish looks as if it has a fluffy coat on. It scratches continually and shows movements of irritation.	As above.
Constipation or Indigestion	Fish is inactive; its abdomen bulges.	One tblsp. of Epsom salt in 5 gallons of water. Let fish fast for 4 days, then feed only live or frozen foods for one week.
Fish Lice *(Argulus)*	Violent rubbing to rid itself of parasite. A light green area about 1/8 inch in size will be noticed.	15-minute bath in a light pink solution of potassium permanganate. Remove parasite by placing a match on it or drip paraffin on it. Paint region with 5% methylene blue solution. Repeat paint job in 12 and 24 hours.

Diseases

Even though this goldfish is almost completely white in color, it's not considered to be a true albino, as it does not have red or pink eyes.

Name	Symptoms	Treatment
Anchor Worm (*Lernaea*)	Violent rubbing; scabs form; a white worm protrudes.	As above. Make sure you pick the worm out by its base, checking to see if you have the anchor. Disinfect your tank.
Dropsy	Bloated body; scales stand on end.	No known cure. Try a warm salt water bath for a day. If no response, destroy specimen.
Ich (*Ichthyophthirius*)	Fine white spots extending over body and fins.	5 drops of 5% methylene blue per gallon. Keep fish in it for one week. 4 drops of 2% Mercurochrome used instead of 5 drops of methylene blue.
Fin Rot or Tail Rot	Bad shredding of tips of fins, gradually moving inward. Shredding starts at edge and works in.	5-minute dip in a solution of 8 crystals of potassium permanganate to 3 quarts of water. Cut off ragged portion of fin with razor blade; paint stub with 5% methylene blue.
Fin Congestion	Blood vessels in fins become red and swollen. Later fins begin to split.	1 tblsp. rock salt in 1 gallon of water; fast fish in this for 4 days.
Fungus (*Saprolegnia*)	Fluffy white patches over body and fins.	1 tsp. salt in 3 quarts of water; keep fish in this one week, changing solution daily. One drop per gallon of 5% methylene blue—keeps fungus off eggs. Malachite green solution sold in stores.

Diseases

If light is used effectively, one can capture on film the iridescent quality of the scales.

Name	Symptoms	Treatment
China Disease	Varying from fraying or split fins which start near the base and work out to fin edge; sometimes blackening of fins and ventral region.	No known cure. Destroy fish and disinfect tank. Highly contagious.
Swim Bladder Problems	Fish, especially fancy ones, turn upside down with belly up.	If a female, it could be spawn binding. Rid her of eggs by pressing lightly on abdomen, working fingers toward anus. If not this, try a mild salt bath (1 tsp. per gallon). Many times this rights itself.

Black pigmentation is commonly seen among goldfish.

Breeding

If you decide to breed goldfish, you must know something about that branch of biology known as genetics which deals with heredity and variation. During the last 40 years Professor Chen of China, Dr. Matsui of Japan, and Dr. Affleck of Great Britain have done much to clarify the confusing mass of facts concerning the heredity of goldfish.

Even before genetics became the vogue, Dr. Matsui set up a breeding schedule to stagger the imagination. Through thousands of spawnings he established a goldfish evolution flow which has stood the test of time.

Upon examining Matsui's work, you will notice two differently indicated lines. The solid lines represent direct mutations from the previous form. As an example: the first double-tailed mutation occurred in the common fish and, being selected for this, produced a strain known to the Japanese as the wakin, a long-bodied fish with a short double caudal fin. The dotted lines represent crosses where one type has been mated with another type. An example of this is the calico ryukin, which is said to be the product of a ryukin crossed with a sanshoku-demekin (calico telescope). The ranchu prototype had no hood, but the general body shape and finnage of the three that followed it looked basically like the osaka ranchu variety present today. The nankin has a fuller body and the downward-type tail.

When breeding goldfish, there are several things that will happen regularly, and for these we have a genetic explanation. Tail form tends to breed fairly true, and for that reason any fish that does not have a completely split caudal should not be bred. If a parent lacks an anal, this will probably show up in the next generation. A

Newly laid goldfish eggs are
sticky and adhere to the leaves of
fine-leaved plants.

few broad generalizations
can be made as to those
traits inheritable most of the
time. In goldfish there is a
constant tendency toward
reversion. A fancy goldfish
can produce all culls if bred
improperly or if it is just
not a good breeder. The
single caudal, dorsal fin, and
elongated bodies will usually
be dominant over any
change from the normal
common goldfish.

This leads us to the terms
dominant and *recessive.*
These genetic terms are
used with goldfish but with
some reserve. Because so
many things can happen it
is best to say that the
majority will occur
according to genetic theory.
As an example:

On April 8 a female (0)
calico comet with black
eyes and nacreous body
was crossed with a male
(o) orange lionhead which
belonged to the metallic
scale group. If we take
RR to mean metallic, Rr

for nacreous, and rr to
represent matt, we can
illustrate it so:

♀ Rr x ♂ RR —P$_1$
(meaning parent
generation)

This cross should produce
50% metallics and 50%
nacreous because if blocked
out it reads as:

	R	R♂
R	RR	RR
♀r	Rr	Rr

In actuality 35 metallic
comets were produced with
35 nacreous comets with
black eyes, 10 nacreous
comets with one black and
one metallic eye, and 3
nacreous comets with
metallic eyes. The ratio of
35:48 is not bad and
illustrates this point. It
should be noted that *all* the

The famed tosakin, or goldfish in Tosa, with the long, upheld tail.

fish exhibit a comet body and finnage (single-tail), have a dorsal fin, and have developed no hood after eight months of observation.

With something like telescope eyes, the normal eye is dominant, and a cross between a telescoped fish and a normal fish will usually produce normal-eyed fish which when bred in turn will prove that they were only apparently normal-eyed. This can be explained by considering two generations.

The word *homozygous* describes the type that has both factors the same, while *heterozygous* denotes the type which has one factor of the recessive and one factor of the dominant. If *EE* is used as the homozygous dominant trait of eyes, then *ee* represents the homozygous recessive trait of globe (telescope) eyes. As stated before, the heterozygote *Ee* has the dominant normal eye factor and therefore appears like a

Artificial plants require less care than do live plants. Wash them periodically to remove algae.

Breeding

normal eye. Using the steps we set up before, our chart is as follows:

P, (Parents)
normal globe-eye
EE × ee

	E	E
e	Ee	Ee
e	Ee	Ee

F, generation

F, (from P, cross)
all Ee (normal eyed)
Ee × Ee

F,' (fry from F, cross)
normal 25% EE | heterozygous 50% Ee | homozygous globe-eye 25% ee

	E	e
E	EE	Ee
e	Ee	ee

F, generation

Proper know-how in selecting the right breeders takes time and experience. Follow a set of standards in choosing the ones which best approach the ideal, and you stand a good chance of getting some better fish which, when bred, will produce offspring that may be even better. The coloration and body shape cycle in goldfish is about five years. Therefore it will take at least six generations (six years) before you know if you are on the right track. This is one reason why it is better to work with only one variety, trying different crosses.

Genetics is a highly complicated affair and certainly not one which can be gone into very thoroughly in a book this size. For further information or answers to specific questions our suggestion is that you consult the more detailed treatises on goldfish breeding which your dealer can recommend.

For each pair of fish being bred, you will need at least four tanks of 20-gallon capacity and one tank of at least 30-gallons. Thoroughly disinfect all of these tanks with a strong potassium permanganate solution or an ammonia solution if the ammonia does not contain detergent. When this has been done, place the 30-gallon in a spot where

Breeding

An attractively colored fringe tail (*top*). In common varieties (*bottom*), color tends to be symmetrical.

the first morning rays of the sun will strike it. Fill it up, add two tablespoons of salt, and let it stand. This will be your isolation and spawning tank.

Next prepare the four 20-gallon tanks, placing them in indirect light. Fill them about three-quarters full. I have found that covers over the tanks minimize the dust that accumulates on the bottom. This is vital for the fry because if too much accumulates the alevins can suffocate when they rest below. Heaters are necessary if you want to control the alevins' hatching time.

The next step is to select the pair which you desire to breed. Keep in mind the standards you have set, and under most circumstances do not choose any with poorly divided caudals or missing anals. Goldfish mature at one year but are in their prime about their third year. Some breeders prefer a two-year-old female

with a three-year-old male; others say size should be considered; still another group recommends trios. I have tried all three methods and have come to the conclusion that there is little difference.

A male that is ready to spawn usually has tubercles or pearl organs, hard epidermal (skin) growths about pin-head in size. The tubercles usually appear on the operculum and first ray of the pectoral fin, but many times they can be found on other fins. It is possible that some males will not develop them, and under unusual circumstances some females have been known to sprout them. In nacreous and matt fish the testis, a long white organ, can be observed in the male fish just above the coiled intestines, which are brown. Some breeders say that during the breeding season (spring and summer) the male's body is elongated and narrows near the tail. If you turn the fish over you

Breeding

Be careful not to crowd your tank
with too many decorations and
always remember to wash them
thoroughly before placing them
into the tank.

may notice that the anal region in a male is elongated and very distinct.

The female fills out during the breeding season, making shape the primary method of sexing her. In matt and nacreous goldfish, the granular yellow ovaries loaded with eggs can easily be observed. The female's body becomes rounded and, especially in long-bodied varieties, lopsidedness will be spotted. The anal region is ovoid and not very distinct. Once you are pretty sure she is a female with roe, feel her belly and check if it is soft and firm. A firm feeling tells you that she is almost ready to spawn.

Once the pair has been chosen, give them a dip in light pink solution of potassium permanganate for three hours. Maintain them in your 30-gallon tank for five days but keep them separated with a divider. Repeat this treatment five days later; in the meantime

disinfect the 30-gallon and refill it with water from one of the 20-gallons. Refill this 20-gallon tank so it is ready for use later. Continue to keep the two fish separated in a dimly lit area. Feed them plenty of live food and vegetable matter but do *not* feed them powdered or flaked foods. Temperature should vary from 70°F. during the day to 50F. at night. After one week of this conditioning, take out the divider and add the spawning grass. An excellent spawning media is a nylon spawning mop; it should be rinsed and sterilized before being placed in the tank.

You will notice a few false starts, but after a day or two the spawning chase will begin in earnest. After driving the female for two or three hours, the male begins bumping her abdomen. If she is ready, eggs will spurt out and adhere to the first thing they touch. They are

The ideal telescope goldfish should be short in body, and its fins should be long and symmetrically paired.

usually released in batches, the first batch being the best. The buck (male) fertilizes the eggs immediately by spraying milt over them. Good-sized females will lay from 500-1000 eggs a spawn.

Remove the eggs immediately and rinse them in a bucket of aged water of the *same* temperature. (Important: goldfish spawn as the water warms in the morning sun, so be standing by when the first morning rays of sunlight strike the tank.) After a quick rinse place the eggs in the 20-gallon tanks, distributing them so that there are about 15 eggs per gallon of water.

At this point raise the temperature in the holding tanks to about 70°F. The **fish will hatch in three to four days. By the end of the first day you will notice some eggs are clear tan to yellow while others are white. Those which are almost clear are fertile; the**

others are infertile and will probably be attacked by fungus. The fungused eggs should be removed without delay. Some breeders have luck with a few drops of methylene blue in these tanks to cut down the occurrence of fungus.

The alevin hatches out along the region of his back, pulling his tail out first, then moving it quickly to release his head. At birth he is about a sixteenth to an eighth inch long and has two large black eyes, a long notochord, and a full yolk sac. These transluscent fry should not be disturbed. Don't be alarmed if they fall to the bottom. Within 48 hours after hatching they will have absorbed their yolk sacs and an air bladder and rudimentary pectoral fin will become noticeable.

Breeding

The feeding schedule should be as follows:

After 48 hours	Crushed yolk of hardboiled egg and oatmeal paste or, for the beginner, fry liquid as produced commercially.
After 2 weeks	Baby brine shrimp and infusoria.
After 3 weeks	Powdered foods can be added.
First 4 weeks	Feed 3 times daily.
Up to 4 months	Feed 2 times daily.
After 4 months	Once a day.

(Feedings should be as much as they can eat in 20 minutes.)

Always siphon off excess food, taking care not to draw up any fry. Once a month add a tablespoon of salt to the tank. Artificial aeration can be provided after one month. At one month cull down to 30 fry in each tank, discarding any fish which are misshapen in body or finnage. This culling should be done with a spoon or cup, *never* with a net. When the fish have reached half-inch, they should be separated into two sizes. The faster growers will starve the others if they are not taken away. When the fish reach one inch they should be culled for body shape and split finnage. This time the thinning should leave six to eight fish in each tank. Cull at the end of four months, leaving only three fish in each tank. At the age of one year, the final cull takes place, picking the four best who will become your breeders for the following year.

It has been said that alga-filled water and feeding starches to fry which develop hoods later on retard or even suppress the growth of the hood. Live foods are to be preferred, along with clear water.

Mr. F. L. Vanderplank of Great Britain recommends a

A beautiful outdoor goldfish pond. Many varieties of goldfish are at their best in outdoor ponds.

color formula of: one crystal of manganese sulphate, one crystal of nickel sulphate, one crystal of potassium bichromate, and a tiny portion (half the size of a rice grain) of copper sulphate, all dissolved in a quart of water, mixing well. Two or three drops (no more) of this solution added per ten gallons of water every two weeks are supposed to bring out the color of the fry. A slightly alkaline tank toughens the fry's skin, making it hardier.

Young fish which have not grown to at least two inches by October should be wintered indoors. Some breeders take in their best specimens and first year fish so that they can be carefully watched.

Experimentation is important at all times because different parts of the world present varying conditions and climates. It will be necessary for you to learn by experience the breeding methods which are best for you.

Artificial spawning is not for the novice. It has both advantages and disadvantages. Professional breeders disagree on its use. Until you have mastered the techniques of natural spawning, don't even attempt any artificial method.

Outdoor Ponds

The topic of outdoor ponds for goldfish is big enough to require a full-sized book. We mention them at all only because goldfish are the usual denizens of these pools. Almost all the varieties can be kept outside during the breeding season. A breeding-size goldfish should be outside for at least two months a year. This gives them the needed vigor they can acquire in no other way. In fact, if you do not want to spawn your goldfish in tanks, just leave them in an outdoor pond and nature will take its course.

Aquatic plants, water lilies, and bog plants all add to the glamor of a well-stocked and planned garden pool. Night varieties of water lilies and tall lotus plants give goldfish an environment well suited for their health.

Fish should not be wintered in any pond less than three feet deep; it should never be so shallow that the water can freeze solidly at the bottom.

Besides goldfish, the golden orfe and Crucian carp provide interesting additions to an outside pond. The Japanese koi or higoi is another type of fish with interesting colors. Although body-shape mutations of the koi have not yet occurred, their coloring far surpasses that of goldfish. People with outdoor ponds should seriously consider adding this attractive variety to their pools.

Index

THE ABC'S OF
GOLDFISH
KW-153